The prevention of plastic and cheque fraud revisited

by

Michael Levi and Jim Handley

A Research and Statistics Directorate Report

Home Office
Research and
Statistics
Directorate

London: Home Office

Home Office Research Studies

The Home Office Research Studies are reports on research undertaken by or on behalf of the Home Office. They cover the range of subjects for which the Home Secretary has responsibility. Titles in the series are listed at the back of this report (copies are available from the address on the back cover). Other publications produced by the Research and Statistics Directorate include Research Findings, the Research Bulletin, Statistical Bulletins and Statistical Papers.

The Research and Statistics Directorate

The Directorate consists of Units which deal with research and statistics on Crime and Criminal Justice, Offenders and Corrections, Immigration and General Matters; the Programme Development Unit; the Economics Unit; and the Operational Research Unit.

 The Research and Statistics Directorate is an integral part of the Home Office, serving the Ministers and the department itself, its services, Parliament and the public through research, development and statistics. Information and knowledge from these sources informs policy development and the management of programmes; their dissemination improves wider public understanding of matters of Home Office concern.

First published 1998

Application for reproduction should be made to the Information and Publications Group, Room 201, Home Office, 50 Queen Anne's Gate, London SW1H 9AT.

Acknowledgements

We were assisted by so many people in the course of this review that it seems otiose to single out any particular ones. Nevertheless, the laws of proportion require us to make these invidious distinctions. On the industry side, with which we have been most concerned here, we therefore express our most sincere thanks to John McVitie of the Association for Payment Clearing Services (APACS) and all his colleagues in the Fraud Prevention Department there; to Robert Littas of Visa International; Brian Bayliss (then of Europay); to all the committee members of the Plastic Fraud Prevention Forum, representing all the major card issuers, card schemes and merchant acquirers; to Alan Hilton and Pat Crowfoot of the Credit Industry Fraud Avoidance System (CIFAS); to Lyn Porter of Experian and to Martin Brassell and Sid Laws of Transax Equifax; and by no means least, to Elizabeth Stanton-Jones and retail card issuer and merchant colleagues at the British Retail Consortium. On the policing side, Superintendent Peter Ackerley from North Wales performed sterling service as ACPO representative on the steering committee. In alphabetical order, we also got special help from Tony Drain (City of London), Peter Jenkins (South Wales), Bryn Jones (Merseyside), Chris Luke (Avon and Somerset), John Newton (Metropolitan), Alfie Quinn (formerly Metropolitan and now US Secret Service) and Tim Salt (West Midlands) and their colleagues.

Finally, we are grateful to colleagues on the Home Office steering committee–Kathy Casey, Paul Ekblom, Chris Lewis, John McVitie, Anne-Marie MacDonald, Peter Ackerley and Ken Pease–who tried to keep us on the straight and narrow and therefore must accept total responsibility for any errors in our work!

It is all too rare for criminologists to get the opportunity to return to the scene of their initial crime prevention efforts: we hope that the text that follows will justify our all too brief efforts, distilled from a much larger body of analysis, and will help to put into rational perspective a set of issues that is commonly treated with abysmal superficiality in the mass media. Even among those who subscribe to the general principle that fraud is not a competitive issue, there will inevitably be conflicts of economic interest within and between industry sectors. Partnership in crime prevention and policing does not magically resolve those conflicts: it offers a set of values which can be used to mitigate them in the interests of the general public and the long-term profit of industry as a whole. This has been a stimulating and difficult exercise for us and we hope that it will give pause for thought not just in the plastic card industry but elsewhere, justifying not only the time and effort put in by business people and the police, but also our absences from our long suffering families.

MICHAEL LEVI, Professor of Criminology, Cardiff University
JIM HANDLEY, Lecturer in Psychology, University of Glamorgan

Foreword

In 1991, 'plastic' fraud–involving cheque and credit cards–stood at a high of £165.6 million. In that year a Home Office funded study, led by Professor Levi (Cardiff University), identified a range of preventive strategies. Most of these were subsequently implemented by the banking industry and other stakeholders. By 1996 plastic fraud had fallen to £97.1 million. In proportional terms, the picture was even better, when allowing for increasing card usage over this period: fraud levels dropped from 0.31 per cent to 0.09 per cent of card turnover.

APACS - the Association of Payment Clearing Services, representing banks and building societies at the heart of the UK payments industry–had been closely involved with planning and implementing the preventive strategies. APACS was keen for an objective assessment of how far these strategies could claim credit for the substantial fall in fraud described above. Bearing in mind the more recent rise in new types of fraud (such as 'credit card not present', when orders are taken over the telephone) there was alsoconcern to look ahead to future risks and to the industry's capacity to 'gear up' against innovative crime.

The research reported here describes the implementation of the 1991 report's recommendations, assesses the contribution of the preventive measures to the subsequent fall in fraud, and looks to future risks and how to address them. The research was again led by Professor Levi. In a fruitful collaborative venture, APACS provided the funds and the Home Office Research and Statistics Directorate assured quality and independence of the findings, principally through chairing a steering group, on which an independent academic, Professor Ken Pease of Huddersfield University, also sat.

The report concludes that the successful reduction in plastic fraud can largely be attributed to the preventive measures taken. However, it also observes that the price of fraud prevention is eternal vigilance, including the ability to respond flexibly to fraudsters' strategies within the ever-changing limits posed by cost-effectiveness.

CHRIS LEWIS
Head of Offenders and Corrections Unit
Research and Statistics Directorate
March 1998

Contents

The prevention of plastic and cheque fraud revisited

Introduction

When Michael Levi-the primary author of this report-was commissioned in 1990 to carry out a study of the prevention of cheque and credit card fraud, financial institutions were about to experience the highest ever levels of plastic fraud to date: £165 million, a dramatic rise from £69.3 million only three years earlier. As a component of the level of UK retail bank bad debt from commercial and personal lending-averaging over £4 billion a year during the 1990s - bank and building society losses from cheque and plastic fraud were then and remain relatively modest. For retailers, plastic fraud is an even smaller proportion of their total losses from crime and bad debt, with implications for the priority that they would 'naturally' give to reducing it. However, both 'government' (in the broad sense of that term, including police) and the private sector[1] saw cheque and plastic fraud:

- as an area of potentially avoidable loss for victims, who comprise mostly financial institutions but include also retailers and individuals;[2]

- area of gain for criminals that might be used to fund other types of crime, including 'criminal capital' for wholesale narcotics purchases;[3] and

- from a police perspective, as an unnecessary drain on police resources, in the sense that better prevention would enable the police to focus time (including paperwork time) on other activities.

In 1990, neither government nor the public appreciated how little plastic fraud the banks and other card issuers reported to the police, nor how

---

1   We are not suggesting that either public or private sectors are homogeneous in their attitudes: we are summarising here what interviews and other sources would show were dominant tendencies.
2   In Britain, by contrast with some other European countries and Australia, the maximum that cardholders can be expected to contribute is £50, except where either cardholder fraud or gross negligence (such as leaving the PIN with the card, or demonstrably waiting for days between discovery that the card is missing and reporting) is reasonably suspected. In practice, even this £50 is waived, partly due to competitive 'customer care' marketing. The Code of Banking Practice states (para. 4.14 to 4.16):
    'If your card is misused before you tell us of its loss or theft, or that someone else knows your PIN, your liability will be limited to a maximum of £50, unless you act fraudulently or with gross negligence.
    Where a card transaction is disputed, we have the burden of proving fraud or gross negligence or that you have received your card. In such cases we would expect you to co-operate with us and with the police in any investigation.
    If you act fraudulently you will be liable for all losses. If you act with gross negligence which has caused losses you may be liable for them. This may apply if you fail to follow the safeguards set out in section 4.8.'
3   Besides, officialdom normally regard 'crimes' as bad in themselves rather than looking at social redistribution costs and benefits: a consistent focus on the latter might generate a radically different set of policing policies.

complex were the national and international relationships between the commercial actors involved. Since the earlier study, there have been some changes in the nature of the 'crime control market' which we will summarise later, but the basic elements of the structure remain as they were. The commercial actors currently include:

- card issuers–general banks and building societies with a major High Street presence

- branch-less specialist card issuers (such as First Direct and MBNA)

- retail store-card issuers (covering stores ranging in typical shopper status from Argos and Dixons to Harrods and Selfridges) offering 'instant credit' and hoping for customer loyalty

- credit reference agencies–principally Equifax and Experian (formerly CCN)–who, alongside the not-for-profit CIFAS (Credit Industry Fraud Avoidance System), vet credit applications for evidence of fraud

- the banks who 'acquire' merchants and charge a fee in exchange for processing their transactions and in effect lending the money to them

- the global card networks–Visa and MasterCard–with smaller volume players such as American Express and Diner's Club, who process transactions and provide add-on risk (including fraud) prevention services

- national card networks, such as Switch, which do not have an international capacity

- third-party card transaction processors, such as FDR, who deal with merchant data on behalf of acquirers

- the retailers, great and small

- the data broadcasters, who send information about lost and stolen cards electronically to the stores' terminals

- lawful cardholders and

- fraudsters and the chain of offenders–including thieves, burglars, 'fences', dishonest merchants, plus drugs dealers and other 'expenditure outlets'– who connect with them.

Although it is not appropriate for us as researchers to set out any ideal configuration of commercial relationships, the interaction between (a) the outcome of the free development of services in a 'market society' and (b) the behavioural opportunities for those who are motivated to defraud is necessary to any proper understanding both of patterns of plastic and cheque fraud and of what can be done about the levels of fraud. In this sense, the organisation of society and, in particular, of commercial practices creates the environment which makes crime possible or even positively attractive. Such a view is consistent with the classic 'routine activity' perspective of Cohen and Felson, (1979)-later modified to include a greater stress on situational motivation elements (Clarke, 1997; Clarke and Homel, 1997)-that there are three core components that determine crime levels:

- the availability of suitable targets

- the absence of capable guardians

- the presence of motivated offenders.

We do not subscribe to the view that 'situational opportunity' is always the most illuminating or even the most practical way of analysing or addressing crime prevention.[4] But it seems clear to us, (i) on *a priori* grounds and (ii) on the basis of a previous study (Levi et al., 1991) and of examples that we will be presenting here, that major plastic card and retail industry players have affected and can continue to affect fraud rates by reducing opportunities to offend. This is partly because *up to a point individually but especially when acting collectively*, they are in a better position to exercise control over the 'criminal market' than are most actual and potential crime victims. In other words, card issuers, merchant acquirers and retailers can act-within limits-as 'capable guardians': some of those limits are inherent, but others are alterable given the appropriate awareness and incentives. We think the 'capable guardians' argument needs to include the cardholder, although some situations (e.g. robbery) might render cardholders less capable than others (negligent loss etc.).

Looked at from the point of view of what potential fraudsters would have to do in order to achieve their objectives (which relates also to the longevity and scale of their ambitions), we may note that fraudsters must

- obtain cards (or counterfeit/virtual reality instruments that will 'pass for' cards)

- obtain with them money and/or goods that they can either consume or re-sell

- avoid whatever penal sanctions they are unprepared to suffer.[5]

---

4   Arguably, some issues require and/or ethically merit more structural 'solutions' than can be achieved by situational manipulation.

5   Though individuals may vary considerably in the point at which their attitudes shift, different levels of punishment are salient at different stages of offenders' lives, and it may take greater punishment once offenders have 'tasted the buzz' from fraud at the beginning. (Conversely, when the 'buzz' is in decline, lesser punishments may still induce offenders to desist.) Judgements of penalty severity vary also among offenders, and between offenders and the 'general population'.

We will deal later in some detail with the mechanism by which cards are obtained, but the most common method has been via the mainstream property crime 'market': In this sense, fraud prevention and target suitability are linked to measures to prevent (and conversely, unintentionally to facilitate) property crimes including principally burglary and theft from the mail, from motor vehicles, offices, homes and leisure areas. The skills of people prepared to offend may determine whether in practice a target is 'suitable' or a guardian 'capable', and this can vary over time: technical 'barriers to entry' can arise for any crime, but what looks like an insuperable technical obstacle at one time may become an easy target at least for some offenders at another, because:

- existing offenders adapt their skills to the new prevention methods

- new entrants with adequate skills come to the criminal market

- previous offenders combine with each other or with former non-offenders in such a way that the crimes become possible.

We might argue that skills are necessary but insufficient determinants of whether a target is suitable, but knowledge and attitudes of both potential victims and offenders might also make an important contribution.

Displacement can take place overseas, where roughly a quarter of card losses are sustained, though this involves effort, cost and a willingness to take risks in an alien legal environment. Displacement risks here may not involve the same offenders: when opportunist amateurs are squeezed out of the criminal market by technical developments, new entrants can come from the ranks of 'professional criminals' or from persons who are educated and/or have a business background, for example merchants who are tempted by criminal opportunities or 'teckies' (technical computer obsessives). Arguably, some technological changes that were quite unrelated to crime unintentionally made some types of fraud easier, at least for a while, reducing the skills barriers to entry for motivated offenders (see further, Ekblom, 1997; Levi and Pithouse, forthcoming). Quality colour scanners and photocopiers, for example, simplify the counterfeiting of *documents* including cheques (which consequently had to be adapted); and (a) widely available encoding machines for magnetic stripes and (b) credit card number-generating and other software readily available from the Internet have had some effect on the counterfeit and mail/telephone order–the latter often referred to in the industry as 'Card Not Present'–component of plastic fraud. As domestic computers become ever-faster and more powerful, their ability to crack routine encryption will rise, necessitating the longer codes that have long been resisted by the intelligence and law enforcement authorities (especially in the US) precisely because it would take *them* longer to 'crack' data, though the ability to decode information does not mean automatically that one will be able to re-program data or re-create cards for fraudulent purposes. However, depending on the discipline and ideology of the 'teckies'–who historically have been inclined to boast of their exploits rather than to suppress them (Sutton and Mann, in press)– breaches of technology can be disseminated almost instantaneously via the Internet, thus generating large *potential* losses in a short time. Our central point is that the inter-relation between fraud controls and offender skills and networks is an ongoing *dynamic* and is unlikely ever to be frozen for long. Thus fraud prevention strategies have to be flexible and build in routinely alternative responses to unplanned obsolescence, leaving the minimum 'window of opportunity' for fraudsters.

Nevertheless, plastic fraud prevention can be expected to generate–and, as we shall show, during the 1990s has generated–a need among those 'willing to offend' to possess higher levels of technical ability or knowledge of prevention methodology than existed at the beginning of the 1990s, and this may reward the smaller number of people who are technologically adept and/or can corrupt those 'gatekeepers' who have responsibility for controlling them. The latter range from (a) retail store staff–who may have knowledge of referral limits (authorisation levels) for payments–through (b) 'computer buffs' who make electronic copies of card transaction data for counterfeiting cards and may try to decrypt and re-encrypt smart card algorithms, to (c) bank staff (including technical support staff) who, under rare circumstances, may find ways of recording the PIN (Personal Identification Number) used in the ATM (Automated Teller Machine) or other methods of 'beating the system'.[6] Nor, except in the final analysis, is enhancing plastic fraud prevention simply a question of changing the behaviour of individuals: collectively, industry bodies (such as APACS, the Association for Payment Clearing Services, in the case of card issuers and merchant acquirers, and the British Retail Consortium, for large and some smaller retailers); their member (and non-member) organisations; and individual stores and bank branches represent a lengthy chain of interests and persons through whom fraud prevention objectives are unavoidably refracted. The *objectives* of fraud prevention may be passed successfully down the chain, but the motivation and the know-how of prevention may be harder to communicate.

This research study has several objectives, including principally:

- a review of what happened to both fraud itself and to the recommendations that were made in the 1991 report, generally known in the banking industry as 'the Levi report'

- an explanation–or as good an explanation as the data allow–of

---

6   We have been informed that banks consider their security to be adequate in combatting internal threats: there is a well-established methodology promoted by APACS which, *to the extent that it is implemented,* will minimise the potential for insider corruption, will generate audit trails should staff fail to resist temptation, and will reduce the scale of any fraud that they may be able to commit.

why these changes to fraud occurred; and

- an examination of likely future trends and whether business people and the police are 'properly' geared up to face those likely outcomes.

In the light of these objectives, it may be helpful to readers to set out what the recommendations of the first report (Levi et al., 1991) were, before launching into the detailed analysis of what was done in the intervening period. For reasons of space in this report, our review of these developments will inevitably be somewhat terse. A more detailed account may be made available through the Home Office Research and Statistics Directorate website.

Credit, Debit and Cheque Card Fraud: Some Key Prevention Recommendations from the 1991 'Levi Report'

Applications for cards

- Merge data sets in the industry, even at the risk of reducing competition among fraud and 'doubtful address' database suppliers. [Largely done, through the Credit Industry Fraud Avoidance System (CIFAS) and credit bureaux Equifax and Experian.]

- Initiate tighter controls over requests to redirect mail, including re-checking requests with customers. [Done, at least in principle, with assistance from the postal service.]

Card and cheque theft

- Continue crime pattern analysis to identify insecure addresses. [Done, to the extent that fraudsters' addresses and other identifiers remain roughly stable]

- Customer collection by or secure delivery to persons living in the areas identified above. [Done.]

- Card awareness campaigns among the public, particularly at work, while travelling, at leisure, and even at point of sale, to reduce accidental loss and theft. Changing habits is difficult, but a useful focus here would be on the inconvenience of card loss, though in practice, this is counteracted by customer service pressures to minimise customer inconvenience. To reduce multiple card theft, people should only carry cards that they expect to use that day. [Vigorous general campaigns in early stages, and more targeted campaigns subsequently. Working out likely personal card use in this way is probably quite rare, and is not encouraged by smaller card issuers to multiple card-holders, who are concerned that it might inhibit spending on *their* card.]

- Cheque awareness campaigns among businesspeople, to increase their awareness of the risks of cheques being stolen in incoming and outgoing mail. [Largely done, though the population base changes gradually.]

- Cardholder awareness of the risks of telemarketing fraud–making orders by telephone or post by providing personal and card details which can be used for fraudulent transactions by dishonest traders–by not giving credit card details on the telephone more often than is absolutely essential. [Done, but hard to achieve full impact without dismantling altogether the use of the service, which is convenient for consumers.]

Card misuse

- Allow customers to select their own Personal Identification Numbers, to reduce the chance of their writing down their number in a document that is likely to be stolen or looked at (even perhaps by people in their own household) with their card. [Done by some issuers, and aimed at by all by 2002.]

- Reduce telecommunications and terminal costs, which are the key to increased on-line authorisation. [Done as a result of industrial bargaining, though costs still inhibit levels compared with Spain and US.]

- Encourage on-line card authorisation mechanisms and technology to vary floor limits from remote terminals, making it more difficult for fraudsters (including store staff) to predict safe card expenditures. [Done, usually with local knowledge, but occasionally with remotely controlled variations.]

- Introduce laser-engraved Payment Authorisation Cards with photographs, which will reduce the number of people who can pass off cards as their own. We cannot be certain, however, that this will bring net benefits to financial institutions. [Done by one bank–the Royal Bank of Scotland–extensively on its ordinary credit and debit card products, but not followed by others after piloting. Cost-effective for some institutions, especially taking into account as savings the private and public sector costs of dealing with frauds. But subject to further falls in implementation costs, probably not generally economically cost-effective for card issuers as a whole, since costs per photo-card are high and visual checking is not done rigorously.]

- Improve staff training and encourage the retaining of suspect cards. Setting 'charge-backs' from the banks for invalid signatures against the individual store manager's performance targets may encourage them to train staff properly. Staff also need greater awareness of what aspects of the card are validated by the authorisation process. [Done as far as practicable, given resources and staff turnover. Charge-backs remain a controversial area for conflict between issuer, acquirer and trader.]

- Tighten controls over merchants by acquirers, checking them against collective 'terminated merchant' files and, if appropriate, obtaining merchants' photographs. Also, continuous monitoring of merchants' accounts to prevent them passing counterfeit vouchers (including those of numbers obtained by telemarketing) through their stores. [Done through vetting by individual merchant acquirers and through the Visa-administered National Merchant Alert service, though technology is currently only beginning to make photos of merchants electronically searchable, and investment in the identification of 'risky' merchants is highly variable.]

Cheque misuse

- Improve security for business cheques, with holograms and other measures to make cheques harder to photocopy and successfully present for payment. [Done.]

- Tighten controls on the opening of accounts and the acceptance of countersigned third-party cheques. Adherence to the Guidance Notes issued by the Joint Money-Laundering Committee and issued by banks and building societies to prevent money-laundering will help this. [Done.]

Policing changes

- Improve regional or national handwriting examination facilities, paid for by banks or police authorities. [Done to a modest extent, due to funding constraints.]

- Regionalise cheque squads, and particularly cheque and credit card fraud intelligence. At present, cheque squads only deal with cheques that are stolen from that Force area, not with cheques that are passed within the Force area but stolen elsewhere. If only criminal intelligence is regionalised or nationalised, mechanisms which ensure appropriate follow-up action are vital. [Not done formally, and informal co-operation is inhibited by funding difficulties. Of those forces that have cheque squads, many simply collate intelligence and have no operational capacity. The exclusive focus of some forces on cheques rather than plastic frauds is also questionable.]

- Include offences of theft of cheque books and of cheque and credit cards, and the fraudulent use of lost and stolen cheques and cards, as separate categories in incident-based crime recording systems. [Done intermittently.]

- Encourage bank-police liaison throughout the country at operational as well as senior level. [Done, though with modest impact due to policing resources.]

- Change credit card voucher system, so that store or bank, rather than fraudster, retains the top copy with fingerprints and good signature. This would make vouchers forensically useful in investigations and prosecutions, and would bring the UK in line with the rest of the world. [Done experimentally, with poor prosecution results–partly because of operational retrieval difficulties–and not adopted outside Scotland, though some multiples such as Marks & Spencer and Sainsbury's retain the top copy.]

There seems to be considerable variability between police forces in their approach to cheque and credit card fraud. The ACPO Working Group set up in the aftermath of the 1991 Report identified six core recommendations:

1. Each force should establish a Force Cheque and Credit Card Squad which should include an intelligence officer and handwriting analyst.

2. Intelligence officers should liaise closely with adjoining forces both formally and through regular regional meetings.

3. Greater emphasis should be placed on crime prevention. In particular, credit card design should use the latest available technology including smart cards utilising biometrics in the longer term.[7]

4. Given the high volume of fraudulent cheque and credit card

---

7   Perhaps the 'latest technology' point is overdone here. Something like CVC2/CVV2 - the addition of numbers on the card signature panel which are not readable electronically - is a very 'low-tech' device which can disrupt skimming operations if used properly. The fraudster can circumvent it without high levels of technological sophistication, but it is a time consuming disruption and that alone may be adequate as a deterrent.

transactions, each cheque and credit card squad should be equipped with computing equipment capable of cataloguing cheques and retrieving information in a standardised format.

5.   The 'Pounds' system of handwriting analysis should become the basic system. There is a need to train every officer as to their responsibilities in respect of cheque and credit card investigations.

6.   [T]he Police Service should actively seek sponsorship from [financial institutions] to fund these recommendations.

In the three years since that ACPO report, the policing of cheque and, especially, plastic card fraud remains far removed from these modest objectives. Only the fifth objective-handwriting analysis and training on basic investigation-is close to achievement. The sixth-the search for outside sponsorship-occurs ad hoc with support for particular operations in relation to marginal expenditure such as cars, equipment of various kinds (including free card magnetic stripe readers supplied almost on demand, which are useful in custody suites to check the authenticity of cards in the possession of those arrested). The banks are using the latest technologies subject to cost and acceptability to major retailers, though many police officers interviewed point out that banks can afford to pay more. However, the other objectives are unrealised. On liaison, apart from ongoing informal contacts and APACS working groups, there are Southern England and Wales meetings facilitated by the City of London police, but as we write, there have not yet been any in the North. On investigation, Strathclyde Police only do reactive, no proactive, investigation of plastic fraud: the very opposite is true of the Metropolitan Police, whose central squad produced a controversial memorandum setting out, inter alia, that they would not do any reactive investigations unless there was an overwhelming reason to do so. The City of London cheque squad-and some others-do both reactive and proactive investigations. There was no opportunity to do any systematic analysis of divisional investigative work in this study-which is concerned principally with prevention-but informal discussions suggest that except for the effects of talks by Cheque Squad officers on how uniformed and CID officers can make use of cheque and plastic card data, only modest attention is paid to these activities in the divisions. The number of proactive investigations into 'skimming' or collusive traders in the divisions is reckoned to be modest by both police and industry sources.

Of the 43 police forces in England and Wales, as we write, 25 have a designated cheque and/or credit card squad-of whom over a quarter will not deal with plastic frauds-and one other expressed the intention of forming one within the next financial year: these, like many headquarters services under 'devolved policing', are under threat where divisional police 'fundholders' are not prepared to pay for their assistance. (See, more generally, Levi and Pithouse, forthcoming.) Only one of these squads had no handwriting analysis facility: the majority have a full time analyst as a member of the squad. However, most of the work done by most squads relates to cheque rather than plastic fraud, and many are engaged in collating intelligence rather than making arrests, suffering the common problem of preparing 'packages' for divisional officers who may have insufficient time to act upon them.

We will now summarise the principal areas of change in fraud prevention over the past six years in the UK–fuller analysis will be made in a later work–and make some brief recommendations about what needs to be done to keep plastic fraud within tolerable limits in future. It should be noted that many of these prevention initiatives are inter-related, and form part of a flexible strategy developed in the Plastic Fraud Prevention Forum which was established in the aftermath of the first 'Levi report'. This strategy contained some short and medium term proposals, most of which–with the exception of the move towards the use of a PIN for transactions at the point of sale, whose time may yet re-emerge–have been implemented. It would be unrealistic to expect total harmony of perspective, since even among card issuers, let alone in card issuer/retailer/police relationships, there are many conflicts of interest and highly variable real and opportunity costs of implementing particular measures. But as a method of 'gearing up against crime' (Ekblom, 1997), the social as well as professional process involved has been very worthwhile, even if it is a model that is difficult to apply in many sectors of crime prevention.

Some existing fraud prevention initiatives

1   In the card issuing environment

- Improved technology and participation within the card industry and right across the credit-granting industry to search out for discrepancies in multiple serial and contemporaneous fraudulent applications.

2   In the card security environment

- Better use of prior experience to identify 'risky addresses' and to deliver cards securely to them or require card-holders to collect their cards.

- Better physical security devices to make counterfeiting more difficult.

- Use of laser-engraved photographs and signatures to make

impersonation harder.

3 In the retail environment

- Better modelling of individual card-holders' expenditure patterns to pick out possible fraudulent transactions made following (i) card theft or (ii) use of genuine card-holder details to create counterfeit cards and transactions, with prompt follow-up calls to card-holders to check that they still have their cards or that the transaction was theirs.

- Increased authorisation levels on card transactions (from 10% in 1991 to 45% in 1996) and reduced floor limits above which transactions have to be authorised to be guaranteed, via financial incentives to retailers

- Better technology to transmit data on cards reported lost and stolen quickly to retailers.

- Better control of fraud committed by merchants, including national databases of 'struck-off' merchants.

- Improved liaison and education campaigns with press, retailers, cardholders and police ('Card Watch').

- Greater involvement of retailers in the planning of bank-led anti-fraud initiatives.

4 In the public policing environment

- Modest efforts to develop fraud intelligence–mainly in the area of cheques–and some major intelligence-led investigations of counterfeiting, 'skimming' (i.e. re-encoding genuine card-holder data on a different genuine card), and 'organised crime' networks.

The net effect of these prevention initiatives has been that charge card, cheque card, credit card and debit card fraud have fallen substantially during the 1990s, almost halving by 1995 compared with 1991 before rising in 1996 to £97.1 million, still less than two-thirds of the 1992 peak. The ratio of fraud to turnover on sales of goods–the obtaining of money directly being much harder and therefore treated separately by us because of the distorting effects of cash debit card usage–has fallen almost five-fold from 0.38 per cent to 0.09 per cent over the same period. Our analysis suggests that these falls have been genuine ones and have not been an artefact either of changes in recording practices or of changes in the underlying rates of crimes (such as burglary or theft from cars) that give rise to the availability of cards to criminals. The savings are shown overleaf in Table 1.1:

Table 1.1: Projected savings from fraud prevention measures during the 1990s

	1991	1992	1993	1994	1995	1996	
Total plastic fraud losses (£m)	**165.6**	**165.0**	**129.8**	**96.8**	**83.3**	**97.1**	
Fraud losses excluding cash (£m)	153.3	153.0	120.5	89.7	75.0	88.8	
Value of transactions (£m)	40,561	47,736	54,643	64,026	75,520	93,775	
Number of transactions (m)	1,095	1,293	1,487	1,681	1,978	2,387	
Average transaction value (£)	37.04	36.92	36.75	38.09	38.18	39.29	
APACS published total plastic fraud as percentage of turnover	**0.34%**	**0.30%**	**0.29%**	**0.13%**	**0.11%**	**0.09%**	
Non-cash fraud as percentage of non-cash turnover	**0.38%**	**0.32%**	**0.22%**	**0.14%**	**0.10%**	**0.09%**	
Projected non-cash fraud losses (£m)							
(i) On total plastic fraud (At the 1991 rate of 0.34% of turnover)	165.6	333.7	379.8	434.3	571.5	665.6	
Difference between actual and projected loss (£m)		**168.7**	**250.0**	**337.5**	**488.2**	**568.5**	**1812.9** (Cumulative savings –£m)
(ii) On non-cash fraud. (At the 1991 rate of 0.38% of turnover)	153.3	181.4	207.6	243.3	287.0	356.3	
Difference between actual and projected loss (£m)		**28.4**	**87.1**	**153.6**	**212.0**	**267.5**	**748.6** (Cumulative savings –£m)

Of the 'cumulative savings' projections, we find the lower one–£748.7 million (rising in subsequent years)–to be more plausible because the growth of low fraud risk ATM use creates an artificial 'benefit' which will increase as they replace cash obtained from bank counter staff. (Theoretically, these cumulative savings would grow over time even if turnover remained constant.) In our judgement, only lack of criminal skills and networks would have acted as natural constraints on the growth of plastic fraud.

It is not easy to assess the benefits from plastic (or other financial services) fraud prevention, because public confidence in institutions and in technology is a core component of banking strategy and profitability, and whatever the level of direct fraud losses (and costs of fraud prevention), confidence is an objective in itself. Moreover, fraud prevention 'piggy-backs' on other technological and organisational changes, many of which would have occurred anyway, making proper cost-benefit analysis more arduous than we have had time for. Likewise, it has been difficult to isolate the impact of individual measures–which tend to be interactive–but our research shows clear fraud reduction effects from Experian's 'discrepancy analysis' in multiple credit applications and from checks on new credit applicants against the CIFAS and National Hunter databases; from secure card delivery; from increased authorisation rates and reduced floor limits; from card scheme anti-counterfeiting measures to prevent simple copying of card data; from the striking off of merchants suspected of colluding with fraudsters and their placement on a 'black list'; from 'hot card files' on lost and stolen cheque, credit and debit cards; and from proactive card issuer identification of 'out of character' card transactions that may indicate that a card has been lost or stolen but not yet reported to them as such. Two illustrations show first, the impact of co-operation between card issuers, merchant acquirers, card schemes and retailers on the level of fraud at the retail point of sale; and second, the impact of secure card delivery on frauds.

Table 1.2: Losses on lost and stolen credit, debit and charge cards (£m)

1991	1992	1993	1994	1995	1996
124.1	123.2	98.5	71.1	60.1	60.0

In 1991, only 10 per cent of card purchases had to be authorised by the card issuers. During 1992, authorisations rose to 13 per cent because floor limits above which authorisations were required were reduced in eight key retail areas, though not in supermarkets and petrol stations because of high telecommunications costs on high volume, low value transactions. APACS administered a fund from merchant acquirers to support the drive for reduced floor limits, extended to 20 major retail areas by the end of 1994; by 1996, 45 per cent of transactions (including supermarkets and petrol stations) required authorisation. The National Merchant Alert Service set up by Visa in 1992, listing merchants terminated by all APACS members for suspected fraud and credit risk, contributed to lower fraud on lost and stolen cards as well as to lower crude counterfeit such as embossing card numbers on white plastic. The Industry Hot Card file also played a significant role in reducing losses: for example, patterns of cheque card fraud dropped markedly when Transax Equifax obtained increasing lists of stolen cards from banks. The impact of electronic 'hot card' blocks is shown by the fact that 'pre-status fraud'–fraud before the card is reported lost or stolen and a block put on its use where possible–rose to 60 per cent of total fraud in 1996, compared with 30 per cent in 1991.

The effects of tighter controls on the delivery of cards to addresses where fraud has occurred before and on postal routes on which fraud is particularly prevalent are shown below.

Table 1.3 Losses on cards not received (£m)

1991	1992	1993	1994	1995	1996
32.9	29.6	18.2	12.6	9.1	10.0

Though savings are much greater where security measures are used by a minority of issuers, there has been substantially reduced fraud on Royal Bank of Scotland cards with engraved signatures and photographs: their cost effectiveness is enhanced by taking into account the cost of action against fraud, reduced disputes with retailers over signatures (which can be retrieved easily from the database), and eliminated tampering with signature strips. In the cheques arena, the Transax Equifax cheque guarantee service (based on hot card files and other screening risk data), improvements in cheque printing, and identification requirements on new account opening because of money-laundering legislation have made an impact, though business cheques still provide substantial opportunities to defraud for those with sufficient nerve. There are also identified positive results from some policing initiatives against high-rate fraudsters, by the use of informants from the underworld and from industry, and by surveillance.

Plastic fraud prevention recommendations for the future

General strategic analysis and recommendations

The price of fraud prevention is eternal vigilance, including the ability to respond flexibly to fraudsters' strategies within the ever-changing limits posed by cost-effectiveness. The mutuality of interests principle embodied in the industry mantra that 'fraud is not a competitive issue' is under some threat from (a) aggressive marketing drives and (b) inequalities in the ratio of contributions to benefits accruing to different card issuers from fraud prevention measures. The latter can produce what one might describe as a 'beggar my neighbour a lot even if I get slightly beggared too' attitude in a highly competitive climate where there is a real risk of loss of market share to competitors–whether bank card or retail card issuers–who benefit from collective fraud prevention arrangements. (We do not wish readers to feel trapped too heavily by economic theory here, but there is here a tension between (a) preserving Pareto optimality–a condition in which everyone benefits from a change–which has been achieved by measures implemented by the Plastic Fraud Prevention Forum and reviewed earlier, and (b) maximising the strategic position of any one company with the goal of long-term profit maximisation whatever the consequences for its short-term profits or for other social 'stakeholders'.)

If the overall benefits of fraud prevention–which measures in our judgement suppress fraud but do not permanently displace it, since fraud levels will soon rise dramatically again if the controls are relaxed–are to be sustained, then in addition to continuing the existing prevention measures set out above, we consider that there are several issues that are worthy of serious consideration by the card industry and retailers. Some of our recommendations apply to the area of focused data collection. The remainder relate to card issuers, merchant acquirers, retailers, the police, and the Home Office itself (in relation to crime recording). We emphasise that–as with the control of disease by immunisation and antibiotics–measures may work best in a variety of combinations, so that one does not rely principally on any one immune device: once breached, the French 'Maginot line' proved useless in the Second World War, and flexible response is needed in anti-offender strategies also, with 'second-phase' prevention methods being developed even as 'first-phase' ones are introduced.

One way of analysing the control problems is to review the ways in which cards or the functions of cards are successfully used by criminals and to suggest measures that can be expected to have most impact on them. These are:

1. Applications fraud

The largest impact is the prevention of multiple applications by the same person or members of the same ring, via the trawling of large data-sets with rapid input of new applications data to search for commonalities and discrepancies. The wider the reach of these databases throughout the credit and claimant industry, the more effective they are likely to be, though the benefits to fraud prevention need to be weighed against privacy considerations and the point at which marginal returns from extra data sources decline substantially is not yet evaluated (and may change over time). In addition to the important co-ordinating role played by the Credit Industry Fraud Avoidance System (hereafter, CIFAS) in warning other credit grantors of frauds associated with a particular person previously, private sector databases such as National Hunter and discrepancy analysis-plus-database products such as Experian's Detect will and should continue to play a key role in the applications fraud arena. Dynamic liaison between councils and credit reference agencies on current vacancies can help to prevent 'empty house' fraud, whereby applications from apparently solid but unoccupied addresses–sometimes with corrupt complicity by local government employees–can deceive credit grantors: these could be strengthened further by data matching techniques using information supplied by welfare applicants to public sector agencies provided that these are preceded by data subject consent to such usage and are processed lawfully and fairly.[8] Liaison with the Royal Mail (over requests to re-direct mail) and with the Driver and Vehicle Licensing Agency (over lost and stolen drivers' licences) would also make impersonation fraud harder. False applications in the names of genuine persons at their own addresses, where credit instruments are later picked up by guile or intimidation (though the latter would have to terrify householders into quiescence if it is to benefit fraudsters for long), are harder to combat except by handwriting analysis across applications. Faster communication of 'hot card' data on lost and stolen cards can play an important role in preventing successful fraudulent applications for retail store cards and other 'instant credit', for which they are often used as supporting evidence of creditworthiness.[9]

2. First-party fraud on an existing, maybe legitimately obtained card

However reluctant we may be to acknowledge that almost everyone is capable of 'succeeding' with one fraudulent 'hit' (though there may theoretically be some criminal justice consequences as well as repayment if categorised as 'fraud'), it is difficult to see what can be done to prevent it,

---

8   Information supplied to Councils that are used for secondary purposes not declared at any time may contravene the Data Protection Act even if used for crime prevention purposes.

9   We appreciate, however, that to the extent that bank card issuers are facilitating an alternative to the use of their *own* products, the prevention of retail credit fraud has a real opportunity cost to bankers.

other than for credit reference agencies to continue to give bad references for previous debt, thereby preventing repeat offending against the same or other credit grantors. Early identification of 'bad debt' and 'fraud' patterns on own-card use–for example, by monitoring spending patterns and other credit scoring techniques–may reduce the size of fraud per card, which is an important form of fraud prevention.

3. Stealing a blank card during the movement/delivery process

The prevention of this has been an area of major success, at least in the UK where addresses can readily be post-coded and audited for theft and fraud risk. Secure delivery and branch-pick up by-passes corrupt postal staff and also addresses that have open access such as blocks of flats and student residences (though sometimes at the risk of bank staff fraud on cards that have not been picked up quickly). Such frauds will re-appear if the system is discontinued.

4. Stealing a card in the course of another crime

This is partly a function of general levels of crime, but we recommend more specific targeting of prevention initiatives–including card-holder education–upon modes of crime commission (e.g. theft from cars) and 'hot spots' in which (a) cards are most likely to be stolen, and (b) stolen cards are most likely to be used fraudulently. These data will have to be collected by card-issuers and then passed on for central aggregation and analysis for focused localised and/or national 'card awareness' and crime prevention campaigns. Although some card-losers may not know or may not tell the truth, it may be helpful for all card-issuers to collect data on whether the cards are lost or are stolen and, following some systematic risk analysis, to prioritise 'hot card' efforts even more scientifically than at present.

5. Finding a lost or stolen card

In the absence of more routine biometric Card-holder Verification (CVM), it is hard to see what can be done about this, other than changing card-holders' care levels. Rewards for finders of cards may encourage collusive first-party fraud (and data would have to be kept, though charging customers for replacement would reduce the incentive to collude). There is no evidence about the extent to which those who find cards use them fraudulently.

6. Collecting card details from merchants and re-encoding

The continuation of existing merchant fraud lists, backed up by proactive analysis of merchanting patterns to review the danger signs of trading that may result not just in plastic but also in other forms of credit fraud. Additionally, end-user utilisation can be addressed by measures against Card Not Present fraud, which seeks 'points of compromise' to isolate the staff member rather than simply the firm involved–a task inhibited by management information that centralises the firm's fraud losses in one location. (Though to change systems to combat this problem alone might not be cost-effective either for the retailer or for the banks.)

7. Counterfeiting to deceive a normal merchant

In the medium term–between full roll-out time of 'smart' plastic cards and their possible decryption and re-encryption at some unknown point in the future–counterfeiting should cease to be a significant problem unless merchants are allowed to key enter transactions or use the magnetic stripe as a fallback, thereby by-passing the chip. High coercivity is important for improving card reliability, and–as in the case of Sky satellite subscription cards where the company had a ready alternative in the case of security failure–it will be important to have an alternative ready in case the chip is compromised, given the speed with which the *modus operandi* of breaches can be communicated globally via the Internet and fraud can be committed on globally recognised cards in places distant from retailer education sites. In the short term, continued training for proper recognition of genuine cards and proper examination of core authenticity features such as embossing will be necessary.

Looking more generally at fraud prevention strategies, in our view, a drift away from the motivation to defraud is unlikely in the short or medium term, unless higher levels of social integration and of legitimate financial services employment occur than we anticipate. Even if more policing resources are forthcoming and judicial attitudes change, plastic fraud will remain a lower police detection probability and a lighter sentence probability than other comparable crimes, though there is ample scope for tying in proactive, intelligence-led policing and better liaison between retailers and police to increase the downside risks for offenders who currently face little more risk than the loss of a readily replaceable card. All control mechanisms are likely eventually to become known to fraudsters, especially if they require widespread training of retail and/or bank staff, though there may be little that the fraudsters can do about them (e.g. the remote alteration of floor limits or the random/systematic checking of transactions in a band below the floor or cheque guarantee limit). Though retailers have a legitimate and sometimes conflicting interest where fraud prevention measures affect their costs and trading patterns, especially in Card Not Present cases where they are charged back the losses but sometimes have insufficient knowledge to make an informed risk decision, we must emphasise that 'ownership of the problem' lies largely with the banks even when the frauds occur in the retail environment. But some of what we regard as key approaches to combating plastic fraud are as follows (in no order of priority and with some internal inter-relationship).

Specific recommendations

1. Action by card issuers

1.1   Proactive monitoring of account behaviour will be indispensable, as the proportion of frauds committed before the card is reported lost or stolen increases further (unless technological developments discussed in the next section disable purchases by persons other than the genuine card-holder, not just in the UK but internationally).

1.2   Develop methods of tying in the card-user more closely to the valid card-holder at point of sale transactions. If we care about arresting fraudsters – both for its own sake (for retribution, to reduce one source of income for organised crime groups, and/or as a tactical means to incapacitate high-rate offenders) and to increase the opportunity cost of attempting fraud, which currently is very low–card issuers should extend Card-holder Verification and the 'capturing' of personal ID details. The CVM (Card-holder Verification Mechanism) may take the form of some biometric– e.g. fingerprints at point of sale checked against those personal data on the new chip card–both to prevent transactions succeeding and to leave forensic evidence for automated search and proof in court.[10] Iris-scans and voice-prints are less useful for search and arrest, since they are not included in police records, but they can be used as a preventative method. If arrest is less important (or if realistically conducted market research demonstrates that there is heavy consumer resistance to relatively intrusive identification technologies), the card industry should explore again the viability of chip cards and some CVM such as PIN at point of sale, though we accept that there may be some 'shoulder-surfing'- or electronic copying of PINs and subsequent obtaining of the cards by stealth or violence.[11]

1.3   Investigate training of telephone credit application and authorisation staff to be sensitive to cues of speech and incongruities of statements and attributes of callers, to help pick out the potential fraudster.[12]

---

10   To the extent that potential offenders expect to fail secure biometrics, they will not attempt to do so. It is not suggested that there should be an on-line link to police databases here: quite apart from any data protection rights this would violate, the whole point of chip card technology is that it permits off-line checking rather than expensive, real time on-line authorisation.

11   We are told this is particularly common in Denmark and South Africa. It is the parallel of the rise in armed robbery that occurred when safes were secured, making the theft of cash in transit the only weak point (for those not sophisticated enough to defraud).

12   Given the increasing use of centralised call-centres, this might become easier, despite high staff turnover, though this emphasises the point that many crime prevention techniques provide reducing benefits over time, since such techniques will inevitably become known to some fraudsters, though they may not be able to do much to combat them.

1.4 Critically test and re-test issuer and acquirer responses to emergency calls of concern from retailers, to check that the banks are responding in the way they say and believe they are.

1.5 Likewise, with data broadcast to check (and have as target objectives) transmission time from cardholder report to arrival on hot card file.

1.6 Make sample queries to cardholders who report late relative to the number and elapsed time of fraudulent transactions on their cards: even if no 'first party' fraud is suspected, it may be possible to check on their prior 'card loss' experiences with this issuer and with other issuers and give them some advice on reporting sooner if there is a next time. Obviously this raises inter-issuer competition questions, but improving the speed of customer reporting must be a real objective, since fraud on lost and stolen cards will remain the major component of the 'plastic fraud problem'. Part of this may also involve industry-wide agreements on charging for replacements–for example, after the second or third loss–even if this does run counter to the 'report first' advice. (If card-holders find their original card subsequently, they can be reimbursed or the loss can be disregarded.) There would have to be some 'trusted third party' industry mechanism for holding data on card-holder losses, or the 'three strikes and you pay' rule could be avoided by simply changing card loyalties. We accept that this is cumbersome, but the UK maximum liability of £50 for lawful card-losers–which anyway is seldom imposed, and absolution from which is actually the focus of advertisement by some card issuers–gives little systematic incentive for rapid reporting.

1.7 'The industry' should be encouraged to continue to refine Management Information Systems (MIS) to enable it to focus educational, situational prevention, and policing efforts on highest risk geographical and business sector areas. Thus, refined data on where–geographically and by criminal modus operandi–stolen cards are most likely to be used and used heavily would help to focus attention cost-effectively on local anti-crime initiatives.[13] The value of the MIS is inhibited for cross-industry measures because it lacks data especially in the following areas: reasons for charge-backs (which vary between card issuers); Point of Sale entry mode (e.g. PAN–i.e. Prime Account Number–key); time of transaction (where patterns may appear); primary crime details such as circumstances of card loss; whether the card had CVM (Card-holder Verification Mechanism) or CAM (Card Authentication Mechanism) and whether or not these were used for authorisation. Data are also needed at the level of store or even individual, rather than the retailer in the aggregate; and about the level of disputed individual transactions, since this can be a key to individual staff members running through extra (often small) transactions after some time has elapsed, and then pocketing the equivalent in cash from purchases. Some of the data will be known to the

---

13   We appreciate that there may be some displacement, but there is unlikely to be total displacement.

merchant acquirer and may result in fraud prevention issues being addressed between acquirer and merchant, but the pattern is unknown to the industry at large.

1.8 A centralised, 'rapid response' group, possibly under the APACS umbrella, should be formed to deal actively with emerging problems. The latter might include (a) pooling cases of 'skimming' and (b) liaising with the police and, possibly, high-risk retailers (though the latter could be done by merchant acquirers). Police might be seconded to such a group, which could be located either at APACS or at the National Criminal Intelligence Service (NCIS), which has a national remit for counterfeiting intelligence. Continuous monitoring of the Internet will be necessary to reduce the risk of 'phantom' firms capturing card-holder details for later counterfeit use, though given that the impact of this may be global, the involvement of the major card schemes (currently Visa, MasterCard, and American Express) is important also. In the future, this might become more necessary still to deal with 'attacks' on smart card systems which threaten not only economic losses to card issuers but also public perceptions of the integrity of the system and a consequent impact on the acceptability and profitability of automated banking strategies.

2. Action by card issuers, acquirers and retailers in the retail environment

2.1 Develop a potential for checking more thoroughly the identity of those who order goods and services in Card Not Present situations such as telephone and mail order purchases. If personal identifiers were mandated rather than being used only when suspicions were aroused–for example, by using the Code 10 authorisation request for suspected frauds–then this might be useful, though general use would make the identifier less safe: at the least, to require fraudsters to be more systematic, they should be required to quote their CVC2/CVV2 numbers from the card. Under current contractual arrangements, such transactions are usually charged back to the retailer if not paid for–even when initially authorised by the card issuer–so very few individual losers are victimised sufficiently often to make it cost-effective for them to invest in preventative technology such as data matching. Meanwhile, retailers should be discouraged from supplying goods to places other than the home address of card-holders, provided that they know what that address is: they currently do so usually at their own risk (with–as stated to us–many computer firms losing £20,000 per annum and some individual mail order firms losing large sums, though others can check customers out on their own sophisticated internal credit systems).

2.2 Enhance awareness of store staff[14] in following card procedures, reducing

---

14   This can be done in partnership between the banks and retailers.

the ambitions of fraudsters' attempts and therefore losses per card.

2.3 Help to identify and generate evidence against staff fraud, which may require video and/or manual surveillance[15] unless circumstantial evidence from analysis of 'points of compromise' is overwhelming and rules out any alternative explanations.

2.4 Incentivise particular activities by rewarding the vigilant and those who prevent the greatest losses, with praise and/or with money. For example, it is inherently difficult to deal with 'skimming' other than through retailer co-operation, and alertness in looking at the card number printed on the card receipt and comparing it with the number on the front of the card itself should be rewarded by more than the normal £50. This will also increase the objective and subjectively defined risks for potential fraudsters in 'skimming'. Although most-precise figures are unavailable-cards are 'arrested' as a result of automated checks rather than following proactive retail staff vigilance, incentives should apply at the point where they are most likely to have an impact, i.e. the actual store staff member, and as soon as possible after the incident: otherwise, excluding any 'just desserts' considerations, if card rewards are used by businesses to increase their income, there is little motivation for staff to do more than merely decline the transactions.

2.5 Increase hot card capacities and more widespread sharing of 'hot card' files.

2.6 Restrict, if not prohibit altogether, PAN-key entry (i.e. typing in card details at the point of sale), to prevent the evasion of smart card microchip protections. Another possible way of dealing with the fallback problem might be to mandate additional security checks if PAN-key entry is used. We still suspect that it might be a considerable period of time before the great majority of retailers (by number, not turnover) have chip-reading point-of-sale equipment. There may also be competitive issues that if the cards do not work consistently in one location, customers may go to others where they do. High card quality is a necessary component of this.

3. Actions by the police, in partnership with issuers, acquirers, card schemes and merchants

3.1 Greater efforts might be made to connect 'runs of use' by teams, for example by fingerprint, modus operandi, CCTV pictures and handwriting analysis as well as by informant-generated data. (Though there may be limits to this, since it is hard-without inside information or surveillance logs-to

---

15   The Data Protection Registrar takes the view that normally individuals should be informed of the presence of monitoring or surveillance equipment, for example by using signs. However, Section 28(4) of the Data Protection Act allows covert surveillance where to inform someone of the presence of such equipment would substantially damage the prevention or detection of crime, or the apprehension or prosecution of offenders, *when there are reasonable grounds for believing that criminal activity is occurring.*

connect offenders who simply work together casually.) To some extent, partly in the aftermath of the first 'Levi report' and the ACPO Working Party, this is being done with cheque fraud, but we are in danger of leaving the greater problem untouched in what amounts often to merely lip service towards a slowly declining sector of 'the fraud problem'. CCTV and other methods of imposing proper audit trails on procedures are important components of this process, both as part of proactive investigations and in persuading local traders to store videos for longer periods than the norm, as has happened on the initiative of the police in South Wales and in an increasing number of other force areas: technical and cost changes in data storage should make this easier and cheaper, eventually permitting digitised scanning of photographic records post-arrest to build up a pattern of activity by suspects. Such audit evidence increases the probability of guilty pleas and further savings in costs and time for witnesses.

3.2 Continue with arrest packages by cheque/bank squads, treating plastic fraud as a significant crime itself, and also appreciating that treating plastic fraud as part of a *system* of financing and organising property crime can yield dividends in intelligence linkages to other crimes for gain such as burglary and robbery. Forces involved in 'intelligence-led policing' may find easy pay-off unlikely unless the card user is the original thief: otherwise, they may have to use the fraudster to get to the card 'fence' who in turn may inform against the original predatory criminal, perhaps following surveillance. However, quite apart from any logistical problems in practice, one might question whether the fence was not more important than the burglars and thieves in disrupting criminal markets, whatever the short-term difference to the clear-up figures for burglary and theft.

3.3 Selective investigation and prosecution policy, including the use of 'sting' operations against dishonest traders, to enhance the risks for collusive merchants and liaison schemes with high-risk retailers to secure arrests of attempted fraudsters at the point of sale.

3.4 There is scope for co-ordinating police, bank and retailer activity by making greater use of local data. An example is robbery where, at least in London, approximately one in five street robbers obtain plastic cards in the course of their taking whatever the victim has. Since the victim knows immediately that they have lost their cards (though the police might have to prompt them with a 'did you lose any cards?' question when the primary crime is reported and get them to find an existing receipt, since many people will be unable to remember their card numbers), not only can the card be blocked very soon, reducing the motivation to rob and the benefits therefrom, but also given that most robbers operate very close to where they live[16] (and possibly spend money close by also), shopkeepers in the area could be given better links to banks and to the police: cards stolen in robberies might be communicated rapidly to merchants on a 'special alert'

---

16   We are grateful to Professor Ken Pease for this observation, and for the robbery data.

basis, and the banks could gear themselves up for special handling of authorisations for those cards. Since those offenders are also high volume offenders–and though there are no data on how many of them use or pass on to other offenders the cards they steal or on how often they do so - their arrest might have a significant effect on levels of robbery as well as on plastic card fraud losses.[17] At the least, there should be a marked reduction in losses per card obtained by robbery and an opportunity for all to demonstrate their concern to deal in partnership with a high-seriousness local crime. Cards obtained by robbery are only a small proportion of the total losses to issuers–we cannot give more precise figures because neither individual institutions nor APACS collectively keep data such as these–but this is an illustration of where card data can be important in crime reduction and arresting offenders. Some controlled experiments along these lines would be worthwhile.

3.5 The original six recommendations of the ACPO Working Group (set out earlier) should be re-examined and, unless there are sound reasons to the contrary, implemented.

4. Action by government

4.1 Implement a rational and intellectually consistent crime recording system which treats each use of a cheque and plastic card as an individual crime, 'debited' separately to each force/division at the point of use: some 'first party' fraud may be legally ambiguous, but it is difficult to see how card transactions made after a card has been reported lost or stolen can be properly classified as anything other than criminal. In principle, the same analysis may be made of unsuccessful attempts to defraud, again provided that the card is reported then or later as having been lost or stolen.[18]

4.2 Further attention should be paid to the amount of resources allocated to the important area of inter-force crime that falls below the sophistication threshold or outside the self-selected parameters of the National Criminal Intelligence Service or the new National Crime Squad, but that requires too much investigation to interest the average divisional or even force CID.

---

17   The chances of them being caught on any one occasion may not be very high, but the more frequently they offend, the more likely they are to be caught at *some* stage.

18   It may be that such frauds are actually committed by the card-holder but this seems little different from noting that some reported and recorded burglaries and robberies are actually insurance frauds. We strongly welcome the current government's moves towards more honest and illuminating recording of crime statistics, and towards the proper recording of multiple-victim frauds as multiple offences. However, even under such a rational recording system, the greater proportion of plastic fraud will remain unreported–because card issuers, merchants and merchant acquirers do not wish to overload the police with cases that they do not expect to have any arrest outcome–and therefore will remain unrecorded.

Discussion

As we observed earlier, there is unlikely to be any one form of control that would eliminate plastic fraud in the long term: from what we know of the culture of offending and the history of crime prevention, experimentation by new entrants as well as by existing offenders is likely to erode the impact of technical prevention over time (see Ekblom, 1997, for example). Moves towards improved Card-holder Verification Mechanisms at point of sale would control the use of lost and stolen cards, because few offenders would have the resources to displace overseas, and because–provided that PAN Key entry of card details at point of sale were strictly controlled–counterfeiting would not be available as a displacement activity. There would obviously be some robberies and threats (as at ATMs) to obtain PINs to go with the taking of genuine cards[19] but provided that the victim reported the loss of the card and that blocking was quick enough, the average loss per card would drop markedly because the window of opportunity would diminish. Biometrics would be stronger still (with threats presumably effective only in the normally unsupervised environment–for the present–of ATMs) as a protective device: fingerprints would have a stronger link ex post facto with police systems,[20] but 'false negative' rates, i.e. the rejection of requests because of system malfunction would have to fall substantially before these become socially acceptable. One consequence might be some slightly greater delays for consumers at check-outs, but the economic consequences of this vary considerably between retail outlets, with some smaller outlets being disadvantaged by fraud controls. When major retailers can offer cash-backs on plastic cards (partly to reduce their own money-handling charges) and banking services at the check-out counter, some might see it as inconsistent to use 'customer resistance' as an argument against delays caused by bank cards.[21]

It is not only retailers who may resist attempts of card issuers to cut their losses by imposing controls. Patterns of 'ownership of space', for example the privatisation of railways, which has brought the policing of trains into a more commercial framework, are important. There have been spates of thefts of one card from wallets in the pockets of jackets hung up in first class compartments (and of the jackets themselves). It has been suggested to us that crime prevention efforts in this context have been less robust because privatised railway companies may be more concerned about the negative 'fear of crime' publicity that is required to get passengers to take precautions

---

19 It is not difficult for planned offenders to disguise themselves against CCTV identification at ATMs, unless some voice-recording (with subsequent voice ID matching)– excluding the PIN–is added, which would also be useable at resolving 'phantom withdrawal' disputes. We have not examined the cost-effectiveness of such measures and this risk may not merit general installation at present: the danger is that it would put users off the new technology altogether.

20 European privacy rights would permit on-line checking against police records in only the most serious of entries (if then).

21 Though the fact that retailers are prepared to sustain heavy losses on their own retail cards rather than give credit processors longer to examine the account and account-holder suggests that concern about business lost through waiting is genuine.

than about reducing crime. This is merely an illustration of the way in which wider socio-economic changes can alter the practicalities of the prevention of fraud and of other crimes. Our study details the ways in which card issuers and card schemes, merchant acquirers, and retailers have combined successfully to reduce plastic fraud at a time of dynamic expansion of card ownership and use: this all too rare illustration of demonstrable medium-term success in crime reduction has been hard and expensively won, with the pending roll-out of smart cards being merely the most visible sign to consumers of industry investment in the credibility of its products. A low end estimate of the scale of threats to commerce should prevention measures fail may be deduced from the number of attempted frauds. Unfortunately, general data on attempted fraud on lost and stolen cards are not kept. To illustrate the actual threat, during 1997, CIFAS – the Credit Industry Fraud Avoidance System – which lists frauds on specific names and addresses on an on-line computer file - had reported 31,107 frauds on banks (of which half were attempts), and 28,221 frauds on retail credit (of which a quarter were attempts, demonstrating the greater difficulties of prevention in this highly competitive sector where credit decisions have to be made very quickly): a rise of 23 per cent over 1996. For the small cost of membership and the much greater cost of staff time in processing reports, members reported direct prevention benefits of £21.3 million in banking and £9.4 million in retail credit from these checks for 1997 alone. One can only speculate on the level of successful fraud if checks were not known by those motivated to defraud to be in place, since there would be little discouragement for criminal expansion.

We anticipate that the level of plastic fraud will again rise significantly above the £100 million mark–and in many respects, the ratio of fraud losses (i) to turnover and (ii) to the number of cards in circulation is a better measure of the impact of such fraud[22]–but we hope that our efforts in tracing the history and impact of these planned responses to crime and risk will encourage a search for collective solutions of this kind not only among all the parties involved in plastic fraud prevention but also within other 'industries' who have fraud and non-fraud crime problems.

Despite the growing popularity of communitarian philosophy and the enthusiasm of some politicians for broad conceptions of who is entitled to be a 'stake-holder' in corporate activities, there are limits to the fruitfulness of crime prevention partnerships (involving perhaps reduced 'primary crimes' as well as fraud losses) where the costs and benefits are distributed unevenly among different parties. It has been argued in some quarters that the police should not be expected to pick up the bill for the fall-out from the risk-management activities of corporations (as in fact they do only to an

---

22   The ratio of fraud losses to card industry profits might be useful as a trigger to enthusiasm for prevention, but apart from any practical difficulties in disclosure of such data, this would need comparison with the ration of burglary/car crime costs to 'affordability' for individuals and businesses, which are not currently measured.

extremely limited extent-see further, Levi and Pithouse, forthcoming). That assertion might have some appeal as a crude way of rationing scarce police resources away from comparatively wealthy victims, but since most forms of theft, burglary and even violent crime arise because of the (intentional or inadvertent) risk management practices of individuals in where they travel, live or go for entertainment, there seems to be no logical reason why the police should not also withdraw from dealing with those offences.[23] Both we and the plastic card industry accept that the primary responsibility for fraud prevention is theirs. But one issue that remains unresolved is what contribution the public sector-principally the police, but also other anti-fraud agencies who possess data that are relevant to credit granting decisions -is to play in supporting private sector efforts at fraud prevention. It seems clear to us that the process of offender adaptations to industry fraud prevention measures and vice versa will continue, and that quite apart from their direct losses to fraud, the financial services industry will have to continue to spend on fraud prevention in order to reassure the public that their investment in high technology banking will not lead to unacceptable levels of risk, including the risk of impersonation of genuine card-holders by fraudsters. The primary cost must fall on the financial institutions-who anyway are in the best position to control their losses-but the centrality of plastic payments to the routines of modern economic life means that the reduction of plastic fraud is a proper part of the problem of security and order in contemporary society.

---

23   In absolute terms, many crime victims-for example, those living in poor 'social housing'-may have little economic alternative to their current lifestyle and area of residence. But many others do have some choice but are not willing to blight their lives by behaving in a totally risk-averse way.

References

Clarke, R. (1997). *'Introduction', Situational Crime Prevention: Successful Case Studies.* New York: Harrow and Heston.

Clarke, R. and Homel, R. (1997). *'A revised classification of situational crime prevention techniques',* in S.Lab (ed.) Crime Prevention at a Cross-roads. Cincinnati: Anderson.

Cohen, L. and Felson, M. (1979). *Social change and crime rate trends: A routine activities approach.* American Sociological Review 44, pp. 588-608.

Ekblom, P. (1997). *Gearing up against crime: A dynamic framework to help designers keep up with the adaptive criminal in a changing world.* International Journal of Risk, Security and Crime Prevention, 2 pp. 249 - 266.

Levi, M., Bissell, P. and Richardson, J. (1991). *The prevention of Cheque and Credit Card Fraud.* Crime Prevention Paper 26. London: Home Office (Police Research Group).

Levi, M. and Pithouse, A. (forthcoming). *White Collar Crime and its victims.* Oxford: Clarendon Press.

Sutton, M. and Mann, D.. (forthcoming). *'Net crime'.* British Journal of Criminology 39/2. Spring 1998.

Publications

List of research publications

A list of research reports for the last year is provided below. A **full** list of publications is available on request from the Research and Statistics Directorate Information and Publications Group.

Home Office Research Studies (HORS)

170. **Understanding the sentencing of women.** Edited by Carol Hedderman and Lorraine Gelsthorpe. 1997.

171. **Changing offenders' attitudes and behaviour: what works?** Julie Vennard, Darren Sugg and Carol Hedderman 1997.

172. **Drug misuse declared in 1996: latest results from the British Crime Survey.** Malcolm Ramsay and Josephine Spiller. 1997.

173. **Ethnic monitoring in police forces: A beginning.** Marian FitzGerald and Rae Sibbitt. 1997.

174. **In police custody: Police powers and suspects' rights under the revised PACE codes of practice.** Tom Bucke and David Brown. 1997.

176. **The perpetrators of racial harassment and racial violence.** Rae Sibbitt. 1997.

177. **Electronic monitoring in practice: the second year of the trials of curfew orders.** Ed Mortimer and Chris May. 1997.

179. **Attitudes to punishment: findings from the British Crime Survey.** Michael Hough and Julian Roberts. 1998.

Nos. 175 and 178 are not published yet.

Research Findings

47. **Sentencing without a pre-sentence report.** Nigel Charles, Claire Whittaker and Caroline Ball. 1997.

48. **Magistrates' views of the probation service.** Chris May. 1997.

49. **PACE ten years on: a review of the research.** David Brown. 1997.

50. **Persistent drug–misusing offenders.** Malcolm Ramsay. 1997.

51. **Curfew orders with electronic monitoring: The first twelve months.** Ed Mortimer and George Mair. 1997.

52. **Police cautioning in the 1990s.** Roger Evans and Rachel Ellis. 1997.

53. **A reconviction study of HMP Grendon Therapeutic Community.** Peter Marshall. 1997.

54. **Control in category c prisons.** Simon Marshall. 1997.

55. **The prevalence of convictions for sexual offending.** Peter Marshall. 1997.

56. **Drug misuse declared in 1996: key results from the British Crime Survey.** Malcolm Ramsay and Josephine Spiller. 1997.

57. **The 1996 International Crime Victimisation Survey.** Pat Mayhew and Phillip White. 1997.

58. **The sentencing of women: a section 95 publication.** Carol Hedderman and Lizanne Dowds. 1997.

59. **Ethnicity and contacts with the police: latest findings from the British Crime Survey.** Tom Bucke. 1997.

60. **Policing and the public: findings from the 1996 British Crime Survey.** Catriona Mirrlees-Black and Tracy Budd. 1997.

61. **Changing offenders' attitudes and behaviour: what works?** Julie Vennard, Carol Hedderman and Darren Sugg. 1997.

62. **Suspects in police custody and the revised PACE codes of practice.** Tom Bucke and David Brown. 1997.

63. **Neighbourhood watch co-ordinators.** Elizabeth Turner and Banos Alexandrou. 1997.

64. **Attitudes to punishment: findings from the 1996 British Crime Survey.** Michael Hough and Julian Roberts. 1998.

65.   **The effects of video violence on young offenders.** Kevin Browne and Amanda Pennell. 1998.

66.   **Electronic monitoring of curfew orders: the second year of the trials.** Ed Mortimer and Chris May. 1998.

67.   **Public perceptions of drug-related crime in 1997.** Nigel Charles. 1998.

68.   **Witness care in magistrates' courts and the youth court.** Joyce Plotnikoff and Richard Woolfson. 1998.

Occasional Papers

Evaluation of a Home Office initiative to help offenders into employment. Ken Roberts, Alana Barton, Julian Buchanan and Barry Goldson. 1997.

The impact of the national lottery on the horse-race betting levy. Simon Field and James Dunmore. 1997.

The cost of fires. A review of the information available. Donald Roy. 1997.

Monitoring and evaluation of WOLDS remand prison and comparisons with public-sector prisons, in particular HMP Woodhill. A Keith Bottomley, Adrian James, Emma Clare and Alison Liebling. 1997.

Requests for Publications

Home Office Research Studies and, Research Findings can be requested from:

Research and Statistics Directorate
Information and Publications Group
Room 201, Home Office
50 Queen Anne's Gate
London SW1H 9AT
Telephone: 0171-273 2084
Fascimile: 0171-222 0211
Internet: http://www.open.gov.uk/home_off/rsd/rsdhome.htm
E-mail: rsd.ha apollo @ gtnet.gov.u.

Occasional Papers can be purchased from:
Home Office
Publications Unit
50 Queen Anne's Gate
London SW1H 9AT
Telephone: 0171 273 2302

HMSO Publications Centre

(Mail, fax and telephone orders only)
PO Box 276, London SW8 5DT
Telephone orders: 0171-873 9090
General enquiries: 0171-873 0011
(queuing system in operation for both numbers)
Fax orders: 0171-873 8200